Michael Jordan
A Team Player

Rita Petrucelli

illustrated by Luciano Lazzarino

Rourke Enterprises Vero Beach, Florida

Manufactured in the United States of America

Library of Congress Cataloging-in-Publication Data

Petrucelli, Rita, 1942-
  Michael Jordan, a team player / Rita Petrucelli.
    p.   cm. —(Reaching your goal)
  Summary: Follows the life of the high-scoring Chicago
Bulls player who could not get on his high school basketball
team because he was too short. Includes advice on setting
and reaching goals.
    ISBN 0-86592-428-7
    1. Jordan, Michael, 1963-   —Juvenile literature. 2.
Basketball players—United States—Biography—Juvenile
literature. [1. Jordan, Michael, 1963-   . 2. Basketball
players.   3. Afro-Americans—Biography.] I. Title. II.
Series.
GV884.J67P47   1989
796.32'3'0924—dc19
[B]
[92]   88-15663
                                                        CIP
                                                         AC

"Dad, hurry up," said Michael. "Larry and I want to shoot some baskets."

Mr. Jordan had just finished building a backyard basketball court. The court was a special treat for his sons Michael and Larry. Michael was 13 years old at the time. Larry was a few years older.

Larry was much taller than Michael. But Michael liked playing ball with his brother. They played every day. Other kids in the neighborhood played too. Michael liked to win. He tried hard to make baskets.

Michael practiced jumping. Every day, he jumped a little higher. Michael's friends called him Rabbit because he jumped so high. One day, Michael would become a great basketball star. He would become famous for his high jumps.

Michael Jordan was born in Wilmington, North Carolina, on February 17, 1963. He had two brothers and two sisters. Michael's parents were hard-working people. They taught their children to work hard too. Michael's parents weren't interested in playing sports. But Michael was.

How did Michael become a great basketball player? As a youngster, Michael was a happy-go-lucky boy. He was a good boy who wasn't hard to please. "Michael was not a born basketball player. He set goals for himself," said his father. "And he worked hard to reach them. Michael's leaping just didn't happen. He worked at it."

Basketball wasn't the only sport Michael played. He also played Little League baseball. Michael was a pitcher. He pitched two no-hitters.

Michael wanted to be on his high school basketball team very much. But he didn't make it. He was too short. So Michael played football, baseball, and ran track. When Michael was 16 years old, he thought he should stick to baseball and forget about playing basketball.

Something happened to change Michael's mind about basketball. One summer, he grew four inches! In his last year of high school, Michael grew three more inches. Then Michael played on the high school basketball team. He was the star player.

Many colleges wanted Michael to play for their teams. Michael felt special. "I felt like someone tapped me on the shoulder and told me that I must do great things." said Michael. So Michael practiced an extra hour a day. He wanted to be ready to play college basketball.

Michael went to the University of North Carolina. He studied geography, and he played basketball.

Michael's first year playing college basketball was a good one. He scored about 13 points in each game. His friends and fans called him Superman! Michael's next year was even better. He scored about 20 points in each game. Michael was voted College Player of the Year.

At college, Michael roomed with another basketball player. His name was Buzz Peterson. Buzz thought Michael was fun to be around. Buzz taught Michael how to play golf. Michael showed Buzz how to shoot pool.

One day, Buzz had to rush home to visit a sick aunt. When Buzz came back to school, he had a surprise. Michael had cleaned the room. He had cleaned Buzz's closet, made his bed, and put away his shoes. "Michael is a real nice guy," said Buzz. "And he's a good friend."

Michael tried out for the 1984 Olympic basketball team. He made it and was elected captain. Michael was an excellent basketball player. But he wanted to be even better. Michael practiced shooting from far away from the basket. His shots got better and better. Michael made more and more baskets. He helped the U.S. team to win a gold medal.

Scouts for many pro teams watched Michael play in the Olympics. They liked the way Michael jumped through the air. They liked to watch Michael score points and win games.

A pro team called the Chicago Bulls chose Michael to play for them. The Bulls weren't winning many games. They hoped Michael would help change that.

In Michael's first year as a Chicago Bull, he scored about 28 points a game. He was named Rookie of the Year. He won an award for being the best pro basketball player that year.

People began calling Michael "Air Jordan." Why? To make a basket, Michael would jump more than 40 inches off the floor into the air!

When Michael goes up for a shot, he does something no one else does. He sticks out his tongue! "My dad used to stick out his tongue too," said Michael. "He'd do it when he fixed the car. I guess I picked it up from him."

Michael is the Bulls' star player. He has won many awards. Michael led the fans' All-Star voting in 1986-87 too. But he hasn't let that go to his head. "I'm just a team player. I'll help all I can to win games," says Michael.

Michael made 146 points in a slam-dunk championship contest. He won first prize. It was $12,500. Michael didn't keep all the the prize money. He shared it with his teammates.

Michael is an easy person to like. He has a lot of fans. When the Bulls play at home in Chicago, the crowd cheers the loudest for Michael.

Every day, Michael gets fan letters. He reads as many letters as he can. Michael and members of his fan club answer the letters. Michael sends pictures of himself to his fans too.

Michael works for big companies when he isn't playing basketball. The companies ask Michael to promote (show off) the things they make. The companies hope people will buy the things that Michael promotes. Two of those things are "Air Jordan" basketball shoes and "Time Jordan" watches.

When Michael isn't working, he relaxes at home in Chicago. He watches video tapes of his games. He likes to bowl, play pool, and listen to music. Michael also does his own shopping and housecleaning!

Michael made 146 points in a slam-dunk championship contest. He won first prize and shared the prize money with his teammates.

Michael Jordan spends a lot of time visiting schools and basketball clinics. He loves kids and loves to work with kids. Michael remembers where he came from. He remembers how hard he worked to reach his goal. Michael wants to make it a little easier for others to reach their goals. One of Michael's teammates says, "Wherever Michael goes, people want to say 'hi' to him. He is one of God's special children."

Reaching Your Goal

What are your goals? Here are some steps
to help you reach them.

1. **Decide on your goal.**
   It may be a short -term goal like one
   of these:
   learning to ride a bike
   getting a good grade on a test
   keeping your room clean
   It may be a long-term goal like one
   of these:
   learning to read
   learning to play the piano
   becoming a lawyer

2. **Decide if your goal is something you really
   can do.**
   Do you have the talent you need?
   How can you find out? By trying!
   Will you need special equipment?
   Perhaps you need a piano or ice skates.
   How can you get what you need?
   Ask your teacher or your parents.

3. Decide on the first thing you must do.
Perhaps this will be to take lessons.

4. Decide on the second thing you must do.
Perhaps this will be to practice every day.

5. Start right away.
Stick to your plan until you reach your goal.

6. Keep telling yourself, "I can do it!"

Good Luck! Maybe some day you will become a basketball star like Michael Jordan!

Reaching Your Goal Books

Beverly Cleary She Makes Reading Fun

Bill Cosby Superstar

Jesse Jackson A Rainbow Leader

Ted Kennedy, Jr. A Lifetime of Challenges

Christa McAuliffe Reaching for the Stars

Dale Murphy Baseball's Gentle Giant

Dr. Seuss We Love You

Samantha Smith Young Ambassador

Michael Jordan A Team Player

Steven Spielberg He Makes Great Movies

Charles Schulz Great Cartoonist

Cher Singer and Actress

Ray Kroc McDonald's Man

Hans Christian Andersen A Fairy Tale Life

Henry Cisneros A Hard Working Mayor

Jim Henson Creator of the Muppets

Rourke Enterprises, Inc.
P.O. Box 3328
Vero Beach, FL 32964